WET LAND

LUCAS DE LIMA

ACTIONBOOKS

Notre Dame, Indiana 2014

Action Books
356 O'Shaughnessy Hall
Notre Dame, IN 46544

actionbooks.org

Joyelle McSweeney and Johannes Goransson, Editors
Paul Cunningham and Jenica Moore, 2013-2014 Editorial Assistants
Andrew Shuta, Art Direction

Action Books gratefully recognizes the support of the College of Arts and Letters
at the University of Notre Dame.

Wet Land
© 2014

ISBN: ISBN 978-0-9898048-2-0
Library of Congress Control Number: 2013957819

WET LAND

Lucas de Lima

These poems mythify the alligator attack that killed my dearest friend in 2006.

To write this book—to inscribe myself into its bloodstained ecology—I have to become a bird.

I transform into the airborne body that shares a dinosaur ancestry with alligators and remains their closest kin.

I do this as if the evolution of scales into feathers were an adaptation to grief.

"*Death*," Edmond Jabès wrote, *"means alliance."*

After discovering that the alligator's blood is so potent it can destroy HIV, I begin to understand our alliance.

Like the Marys—the ACT UP affinity group of the sick, the living, and those who had already died of AIDS—my allies and I spill into each other.

We fall into upper case letters like rows of teeth.

We offer ourselves as this circulation.

Lucas,

Is there any way you could give me a few pearls of advice on my artist statement? I just wrote it now and I'm going to bed without feeling very good about it. I know it's not done, but please, if you have a minute, make comments.

Mutation: [1]

I watched this film from 1959 about a man who transforms into an alligator man because reptilian genes could grow back his missing body parts.

But the alligator man hides his scales from his wife & lurks in the shadows he rises & wilts as many times as a garden.

At the end of the film he even grows the head of an alligator his mother faints his wife cries & chases after him until the swamp becomes a scream the alligator man can't let out.

Mutation: [2]

That's when the alligator man wrestles a real gator & gets sucked into quicksand where muck throbs around his oblong mouth.

The director has to kill off his ugly protagonist & the trapper has to exterminate the gator that got Ana Maria because every story has to end with a period.

UNLIKE A POEM

UNLIKE A POEM I WRITE WITH ANA MARIA

UNLIKE A POEM I WRITE WITH ANA MARIA'S ALLIGATOR

UNLIKE A POEM I WRITE WITH HER BLOOD & THE ALLIGATOR'S

UNLIKE A POEM WE WRITE LIKE A WET LAND

LUCAS, I'VE THOUGHT ABOUT MY "CONTACTS WITH NATURE" ALL DAY, SINCE YOU ASKED IN YOUR LAST E-MAIL.

MARIAS

I DREAMT OF MY MOTHER DYING & WANTED TO BUILD A FIRE

MY MOTHER IS ONE OF MANY MARIAS FLICKERING

IN CIUDAD JUAREZ, ONE MARIA DIES EVERY WEEK ON THE WAY TO A

FACTORY

AS A WOMAN I CALL MYSELF MARIA & WEAR THE DARKEST RED ON MY

LIPS

WHEN I KISS PALE BOYS I TRY TO SET THEIR FACES AFLAME

SO THE WHITE BOYS' CHEEKS MELT

THEN I RECALL MY PAST LIFE AS A WHITE BOY WRITHING IN A WHITE

BLANKET

WHENEVER I WANT TO THROW THE PAGE INTO THE FIRE

ANA MARIA STOPS ME BY CRASHING INTO MY BACK

LIKE A WAVE OF THE VIRGIN MARY'S TEARS IN A LATIN AMERICAN

CHURCH

ANA MARIA WAS THE FIRST PERSON TO GIVE ME A CLOVE

CIGARETTE

IT SET MY LIPS OFF

WITHOUT BURNING THEM UP

ONE TIME MY MOTHER ACCIDENTALLY KISSED ME ON THE LIPS

I STARTED WRITING POEMS WITH A MATCH

THE ANIMAL SITS ON MY FACE

I STARE INTO A DARK CRACK

WHERE ANA MARIA'S BLOOD IS NOT BULLSHIT ON TV.

ANA MARIA LOVED THE FILM *SALO / 120 DAYS OF SODOM.*

OUT OF LOVE FOR PASOLINI'S SHIT-SMEARED CHILDREN

SHE MIGHT'VE SAID

GIVE ME SODOMY OR GIVE ME DEATH.

SHE HELD THE GAZE OF CHILDREN, OF BABY ALLIGATORS

UNTIL ONE GREW UP & KILLED HER.

THE DEATH OF A CHILD IS SO TRAGIC, I DON'T THINK

ANYONE CAN UNDERSTAND UNLESS THEY'VE GONE

THROUGH IT

SAYS THE NATIONAL GEOGRAPHIC ACTRESS WHO PLAYS

ANA MARIA'S MOTHER.

AS I LICK THE ANIMAL'S ANUS

I PRETEND I'M ITS MOTHER.

OH, BOY. I LOVE YOU. WILL YOU SEND ME A POEM?

GIRL OF MY GAY DREAMS

MAKING OUT WITH A REPTILE, I FEEL LIKE RED SKY

MY VIRGINITY SPARKLES IN THE PAST

I WONDER IF HOLES HEAL

I THINK OF YOUR BREASTS & BEGIN TO SCRATCH MY CHEST

I LEAVE ALL THESE MARKS

I WEEP LIKE A MAN

THE SEXUAL CURRENT OF SNAKES IN THE GRASS

WHERE RODENTS RISK THEIR LIVES I GET LAID

I GET LAID &

TWO SWALLOW-TAILED KITES

SPIT OUT A RAY

IF SEX MUST BE LOUD

THEN I'LL OPEN MY MOUTH

I WILL MAKE AN O THAT SUCKS YOU BACK TO LIFE

GOD, DO YOU EVER FEEL LIKE THERE'S A FEATHER FALLING ALL OVER YOUR SKIN, MAKING YOU ITCH HERE, THEN THERE, AND THERE AND THERE AND SO ON...?

O

WHAT WAS THE BIRD'S EYE VIEW IF I HAD NO CROWN WHEN ANA MARIA

DIED IF THE PILLOWY FIGURES SHE USED TO DRAW BURIED SCABS INSIDE

CLOUDS UNTIL RIPPED FEATHERS OVERFLOWED DOWN IF ANA MARIA'S

FRIENDS SPOTTED HER & JABBED THE ALLIGATOR'S PUPILS IF THESE

THINGS HAPPENED REPTILIAN JAWS CLAMPED VALVELIKE I REACH INTO

THOSE JAWS TO FIND HER HEART ONCE SKIN BLOCKS THE VIEW YOU HAVE TO

SOAR THROUGH A TEAR MY SPONGY EYE TEARS OPEN SHE FLOODS IT FROM

INSIDE THE ALLIGATOR.

ANOTHER SUBJECT: I HAVE BEEN HAVING TOO MANY DREAMS ABOUT BEING BLIND.

MUTATIS MUTANDIS

FLYING TO ANA MARIA'S FUNERAL

I LOOKED HARD AT CLOUDS SO THEY'D GET SOFTER.

WHEN THEY GOT BIGGER IT DIDN'T HELP—I PUSHED MYSELF

OFF THE AIRPLANE.

I WAS A PALLBEARER WITH HER FAMILY & HER OTHER BEST FRIEND NICK.

MY BEAK: A QUESTION MARK.

HAD I STRETCHED MY WINGS BEFORE ANA MARIA DIED?

MY HAND: ALL KINDS OF COLORS ONCE IT GREW TALONS &

I PICKED CHILDREN OFF THE GROUND.

"WIND THEM UP."

ANA MARIA DYING GAVE ME ALL THIS AIR INSIDE,

OUTSIDE

BLOOD-STREAKED FEATHERS.

EVERYTHING WAS FUNNY AT THE CEREMONY BECAUSE

I COULD IMAGINE ANA MARIA'S REMARKS.

HER COFFIN & MY BONES HOLLOW

BUT HEAVY.

"GET NAKED."

"GET STUFFED INTO A PILLOW."

"WHOEVER LIES DOWN WILL

EMPTY YOU OUT."

CRUEL NATURE

THE ALLIGATOR IS A GOD UNDERWATER WITH TWO SETS OF EYELIDS.

I BORROW THE DEPTH OF HIS SIGHT.

IN THE NATIONAL GEOGRAPHIC DOCUMENTARY THE ACTRESS LOOKS

NOTHING LIKE ANA MARIA;

THE OTHER ACTRESS LOOKS NOTHING LIKE HER FRIEND.

A SIMULATION OF SNORKELING WITH A DEITY COULD ALWAYS BE REDDER.

ON THE INTERNET I FOUND PHOTOS OF THE MAN WHO PERFORMED THE

ALLIGATOR'S NECROPSY.

A BIOLOGIST IN THE MARINES, HE GLOATED OVER THE 10 FOOT 400 POUND

ALLIGATOR THAT KILLED MY BEST FRIEND.

SO DID THE WILDLIFE AGENCY SPOKESPERSON.

SO DID THE DOCTOR WHO HAD EXAMINED ANA MARIA.

IT IS GLORIOUS TO STAND BEHIND AN ENORMOUS DEAD REPTILE AS A

CAMERA FLASHES ON YOUR FACE.

YOU DELIGHT YOUR CHILDREN WITH PHOTOS OF A PREHISTORIC GOD,

HAVING SLICED THROUGH HIS ARMOR-PLATED SKIN.

THE GATOR LOOKED TOO PINK INSIDE LIKE A RAVAGED DAWN THAT HAD

ALREADY BLED.

O, THE BIRD INSIDE ME SAYS, IT HURTS TO KEEP KILLING ANA MARIA

& IT HURTS TO KEEP KILLING THE ALLIGATOR.

BUT THAT IS WHAT THE HUMAN DOES WITH WORDS

WHEN HE BLOATS & FLATTENS THEM OUT.

IN BETWEEN THE GATOR'S JAWS I TOO SHALL POSE

WITH MY HEAD.

I AM ON ANOTHER PAGE.

A THICK POOL OF BLOOD SUFFUSES THE PIECE OF PAPER

AGAINST A FEATHER ABLAZE ON THE PAGE I WEIGH MYSELF, NOT YET SO

LIGHT;

MY FINGERS TOUCH DROPLETS, SPLITTING THE RED.

NO LUMINOUS HELIX LAUNCHES ME INTO AIR. NO EVERLASTING RAY

PERFORATES ME & FORKS MY TONGUE BY

SCALDING IT IN HALF

& IGNITING THE GATOR DUMMY I CONSTRUCT WITH STICKS.

"OFFER ME A LIVE CHICK," I HEAR THE DUMMY BELLOW, "DOWN DYED THE

COLOR

OF ANA MARIA'S VISCERA IN THE DEPTHS WHERE WE SPUN."

KILL SPOT

MY BULLET CRACKS THE GATOR'S SKULL LIKE AN EGG.

MY BULLET SHATTERS THE GATOR THE WAY A WORD BREAKS OPEN THE

LORD.

MY BULLET IS BEAUTIFUL.

IT SHIMMERS IN THE QUARTER-SIZED KILL SPOT ON THE GATOR'S NECK.

MY BULLET MAKES MY FATHER PROUD.

HE HOISTS THE HUGE GATOR INTO THE FISHING BOAT BY USING THE HEAD AS

A COUNTERWEIGHT TO THE ARMOR-PLATED BODY.

IS THE GATOR A MANLY PINK UNDERNEATH?

I FANTASIZE ABOUT STRIPPING HIS SCALES.

HIS LEG STILL TWITCHES, FADING SLOWLY WITH THE LIGHT

WHEN I SHOOT HIM NEAR THE HEAD AGAIN.

THE BLACK CRY OF A HAWK COINCIDES WITH MY BANG.

I KNOW THE HAWK IS ANA MARIA BECAUSE HER CRY PIERCES

MY EGGHEAD.

I CRY YOLKY TEARS IN THE BOAT WHILE MY FATHER FROWNS AT ME.

THE SKY IS BUBBLING

YELLOW ABOVE.

O FATHER,

I MOAN IN THE CYPRESS GROVE,

O.

ONCE A GATOR INGESTS THE HOOK

WITH THE BAIT OF CHICKEN,

WINGS TEAR THE SKIN ON MY BACK AS THEY GROW.

IT'S HARD TO LOVE REPTILES

IN YOUR AQUATIC CEMETERY,

ANA MARIA.

I'D GLIDE WITH THE CARCASSES BUT THE BUBBLES

FEEL LIKE BURSTS.

TO FLOAT LIKE A LOTUS BLOSSOM, I TURN A MOIST EYE

TO ANCIENT EGYPT.

IT WAS SOBEK WHO PROTECTED THE EYES OF THE DEAD WITH HIS

CROCODILE'S HEAD.

HIS SWEAT CREATED THE NILE.

I PRAY TO HIS SCALES IN DARK WATER THE WAY EGYPTIANS WORSHIPPED

CROCODILE FETUSES, UNBORN & UNDEAD INSIDE

SOBEK'S PRISTINE EGGS.

HE WHO MADE THE HERBAGE GREEN STRUTS WITH A PLUMED

HEADDRESS & A HORNED SUN DISK.

SOMETIMES SOBEK'S RAYS ARE TOO SHARP, ANA MARIA,

A SHINY TOOTH THROUGH YOUR SKIN.

OTHER TIMES SOBEK IS WHOM I CALL ON

TO SMOTHER THIS BOOK

WITH A NEW GAY ICON—

A SACRED EGG.

I WANT TO INCORPORATE THE THEME OF GIVING FOOD, BUT I GUESS I'M NOT SURE OF THE RESULT I WANT TO TALK ABOUT. GIVING TO NOURISH ANOTHER'S BODY OR GIVING AS SELF-SACRIFICE. AND I'VE BEEN INTERESTED IN THE BODY ITSELF AS FOOD. THE CONCEPT OF WEANING OR BEING WEANED FROM THE BREAST.

AVIAN DINOSAUR

WHEN THE BABIES HATCH THEY CRY OUT. THE MOTHER DIGS THEM OUT OF A
WET BLACK MOUND. SHE PLACES HER OFFSPRING IN A POUCH INSIDE HER
MAW. I WATCH & LOVE THIS FROM AFAR, DIPPING MY WINGTIPS IN MUD.

I AM A HERON THROWN INTO THE RING.

THE CIRCLE OF LIFE THAT ENGULFED ME AFTER ANA MARIA DIED.

WHEN A BABY ALLIGATOR SPLITS THE REEDS BELOW ME I STAB IT WITH MY
BEAK & GOBBLE DOWN ITS SQUEAKY LITTLE BODY. I REMEMBER WHEN I HAD
A LITTLE BODY & MY MOTHER USED TO WORRY ABOUT

LIPS THAT ATE CLOUDS

& SWALLOWED MY VAPOROUS BIRDSONG.

NOW THE BOOK VOMITS MY TRIASSIC PAST SO I BECOME, WITH THE ALLIGATOR,

A HISTORICAL BEING

AS THE BOOK EATS ME/

AS I BIRTH MY WAY OUT.

I FLY INTO GOD'S FACE

& ASK HIM ABOUT MY DEAD BEST FRIEND

THE ALLIGATOR IS ON THE SIDE OF THE ROAD WHEN I'M IN THE MIDDLE OF

THE HIGHWAY

I FEEL CONTIGUOUS WITH THE LANDSCAPE

LIKE ANY FLATTENED BIRD WHO SNEEZES BACK TO LIFE AFTER GETTING RUN

OVER BY A TRUCK

I AM LEARNING TO STRAIGHTEN MY SPINE

TO WALK IS TO WALK TOWARD LOVE FOR THE GATOR

ANY QUESTION I ASK GOD ANSWERS BY CREATING A MEADOW FILLED WITH

ORPHANED BEASTS WHO

TAKE CARE OF EACH OTHER

I, LITTLE BIRD WHOSE FEATHERS ARE TARRED

WANT TO GIVE BIRTH TO A BABY GATOR

AN ALBINO

I KNOW THE COLOR OF MY BABY IS IMPORTANT

IT MATTERS WHICH SPECIES I FUCK

BUT IN THE DEAD OF NIGHT

IN THE DEAD OF NIGHT

THE PERSPECTIVE OF THE BIRD IS A BULLET'S

I SHOOT MYSELF INTO EVERYONE

WHEN I PICK SOMEONE

ANIMAL ECLIPSE

GATORS BREATHE JUST LIKE BIRDS IN A UNIDIRECTIONAL FLOW

I PUT MY ARM INSIDE THE JAWS OF ANA MARIA'S GATOR & OUT RUSHES

WIND

OUT COMES MY HAND AS A HIGHLY EFFICIENT LUNG

THE GATOR COMES TO LIFE & OUR EYES MEET

THE SIZE OF THE GATOR & THE INTENSITY OF THE LIGHT DETERMINE ITS EYE

COLORS

I THINK WE ARE GOING TO FALL IN LOVE & MAKE ANA MARIA JEALOUS

SHE IS THE PUDDLE WHERE THE GATOR & I TUMBLE IN A CANDLELIT DEATH

ROLL

FEATHERS & SCALES REMAIN THE SAME THING

OUR TOXIC DIGESTIVE SYSTEM IS ONE & THE SAME POEM

WE RECALL OUR DINOSAUR COUSINS & THROW UP BONES IN A PILE

LUNAR & SOLAR, OUR BODIES EJACULATE COMETS

WE MAKE COSMIC MUSH OF OURSELVES

THE GATOR WITH HIS TEETH & MUSCULAR TONGUE, ME WITH MY HOLLOW-

BONED BOOK THAT BREAKS & MENDS ITSELF IN FLIGHT

UNDER THE WING OF FLORIDIAN STARS WE DO BEAUTIFUL THINGS

TO EACH OTHER

I TYPE THIS AS I AM HIGH. THE HIGHS I'VE BEEN HAVING LATELY ARE OF THE FINEST STOCK—DEEPLY INTROSPECTIVE, SPECTIVE IN GENERAL, LONGLASTING, AND VERY BIG.

SOBEK

THE LIGHT WEAKENED & I TRIED TO BE STRONG. MY MUSCLES IN THE SWAMP
BREATH. I DID NOT WANT TO FALL INTO "LUCAS" & PRETEND TO HAVE LIPS.

THE ALLIGATOR TRIED TO TALK & HIS WORDS WERE A BROOK.

I PUNCHED HIM IN THE FACE.

THE ALLIGATOR WRAPPED HIS TAIL AROUND HIMSELF EVEN THOUGH IT HURT OR
BECAUSE IT HURT. HIS OWN PLATES PUSHED INTO HIM. THEY GLIMMERED A BIT.

O, GATOR, I SAID. OUR UNCOUPLING. THE ARK WAS BUILT IN THREE STORIES. THE
LOWEST FOR WILD BEASTS, THE MIDDLE FOR BIRDS & DOMESTIC ANIMALS, THE
TOP LEVEL FOR HUMANS.

THE ALLIGATOR FINALLY STAMMERED A NAME: S-S-SOBEK.

I KNOW SOMETHING ABOUT SOBEK, I SAID. SOBEK WITH HIS PLUMED HEADDRESS.
SOBEK THE GAY EARTH MOTHER. I HAVE NOT BEEN TO EGYPT. BUT I TRUST YOUR
FAITH IN SOBEK BECAUSE YOU PICKED ANA MARIA. YOU KILLED ANA MARIA &
THERE WAS SOMETHING AWFUL & ARTFUL ABOUT: A DEITY WITH A CROCODILIAN
HEAD. THEY SAID SHE LOOKED LIKE A DOLL IN YOUR JAWS.

FROM THE SUPREME VIEW OF THE KITE, THE ALLIGATOR'S JAWS

CRADLED ANA MARIA

SHE SCRATCHED HIM

SHE FOUGHT BACK

HER BLOOD MIXED WITH THE BLOOD OF THE FOREST IN A GREEN & RED

SCUM

O, GATOR I KNOW THERE IS A HOLE INSIDE YOU SO MUCH LARGER

THAN THE

LACERATIONS YOU LEFT ON ANA MARIA

I KEEP CONFUSING THE BODIES

I DON'T KNOW HOW TO TALK ABOUT

BOTH THINGS AT THE SAME TIME

BREAD & BLOOD

THEY CUT YOU UP INTO

SO MANY PIECES.

I HOPE YOU HEARD A CHOIR AS THE SOUNDTRACK TO YOUR NECROPSY

I HOPE YOU HEARD A LOT OF

GURGLING IN THE WATER

THE HAPPY TIMES YOU HAD WHEN YOU FELT

GREEN IN YOUR BODY

THE HAPPY TIMES I HAD WITH ANA MARIA

WHEN I WAS BISEXUAL & WE MADE OUT, SHE GOT A NATURAL HIGH IN HER

BEDROOM

SHE WAS ALREADY THE BIRD I WOULD HAVE TO BECOME

I'M SENDING YOU A PACKAGE. THE LETTER I'M ENCLOSING WITH IT IS SITTING ON THE DESK NEXT TO ME. IT LOOKS FRAGILE LIKE IT MIGHT CREASE EASILY OR BLOW AWAY.

GHOSTLINES

THE GATOR'S BRIMMING RED EYE DEPRIVES US OF THE GHOST.

MY MUTE WINGS TALK AFTER SOMEONE CUTS THEM OFF.

THEY REVERBERATE OUT OF MY BODY. THEY FALL BACK TOWARD THE

RED SUN.

IF I FALL INTO THE GATOR'S EYES, HE WILL GLITTER WITH ALL POSSIBLE

COLORS.

HE WILL LOSE HIS COLD-BLOODED BLANKNESS & BECOME A HOT BODY.

WHAT ANA MARIA WAS TO HIM.

ANA MARIA. I JUST WANT TO CHECK IN WITH YOU. I'M NOT GOING TO YELL.

ARE YOU THIS BOOK YET?

ARE YOU, ME & THE GATOR ALL

HANGING OFF THE SAME SPINE?

WITH FORMALDEHYDE, OUR BOOK COULD BE PRESERVED AS IT TURNS

BLACK:

OUR MAGNIFIED MEAT BURNING IN SUNLIGHT.

LET US MINGLE IN THE SWAMP A FEW MORE DAYS. THE BEST SHADE FOR

A TEAM TO PERCOLATE & PRAY IN.

WE TEEM AGAINST ALL ODDS IN THE QUICKSAND OF ALL EYES.

ANA MARIA.

YOUR ADUMBRATION.

I SEE YOUR SPLASH OF WATER FROM THE SKY WETTING THIS BOOK.

MANY READERS ARE GHOSTS

OBSESSED WITH OUR BODIES.

NO HUMANS ALLOWED

[POEM SPOKEN IN TONGUES RIFE WITH BACTERIA FROM THE GATOR'S JAWS]

TERRORIST DIVA

ANA MARIA'S CLOSE FRIENDS CONSTELLATE AS NEW BIRDS IN THE SKY TO

TELL ME I'M NOT THE ONLY SACRED FIGHTER.

OK, I SAY. LET US CHANT IN A WINGED PROCESSION UNTIL OUR VOICES ARE A

TIDAL WAVE OF

WE LOVE ANA MARIA EVERYDAY.

ANA MARIA'S FRIENDS NOD, WRINKLING CLOUDS, BUT A BEAM OF SUN

PARTS THE CLOUDS

TO MOCK MY CATCHY REFRAIN.

THIS IS A HIGH-PITCHED POWER BALLAD, I TELL THE SKY.

MY BODY BLOWS UP ON A CRUCIFIX. I NEED A FLOCK TO WITNESS MY

MIRACLE &

A SURPLUS OF FEATHERS TO DISPERSE WHEN I DIE.

MY EXPLOSION MIMICS THE SUNRISE IN LIGHT OF THE LIGHT

ANA MARIA

DESCENDED FROM.

MY NEW SPRING BREAK PLAN IS TO GO TO FLORIDA. I WANT TO OWN SEASHELLS AGAIN, TO LOOK AT THE MANGROVES, CYPRESS KNEES, SPANISH MOSS, CORMORANTS, GREEN HERONS, TREEFROGS, AND SNAPPING TURTLES OF MY CHILDHOOD.

UNITED ANIMALS

PLOP THEMSELVES DOWN.

I LAY DOWN MY CROSS & GUN.

WE ALL BRING OUT EACH OTHER'S BEAUTY, THE ANIMALS & I, AS PIECES

IN ANA MARIA'S ART INSTALLATION.

THERE'S A DEAD GAY ARTIST HOLDING HANDS WITH THE GATOR.

A GOWNED CONGOLESE CHOIR PROVIDES MUSICAL ACCOMPANIMENT &

MORAL TENOR.

BABY APES GLITTER AGAINST MOTHER'S TONGUE.

EVERYONE GATHERS AT THE MOUTH OF A CAVERN WHERE ANA MARIA

IS BURIED:

THE MOUTH OF OUR CREATOR.

AS SOON AS WE TRY TO UNCOVER HER A SPARROW FLITS BY.

ANA MARIA HAS RISEN, THE SPARROW SINGS. ANA MARIA HAS RECOVERED

HER SPINE. ANA MARIA LIVES WITHIN THE EYE OF A TORNADO STRIKING THE

NEARBY SLAUGHTERHOUSE.

OUR MENAGERIE THEN TURNS INTO A MOTTLED ORGY.

BETWEEN FEATHERS & SCALES, WE CELEBRATE

THE HOLY UNCAGING.

I FALL IN LOVE WITH EVERY SPECIES I FUCK.

I CAN'T WAIT TO MAKE THREE-DIMENSIONAL THINGS WITH MY HANDS! IT'S A GIVEN THAT I WILL CREATE SOMETHING FOR YOU.

THE GATOR-ANA MARIA-LUCAS BODY

ON A CRYSTALLINE MORNING OUR BODY CLIMBS A BARBED WIRE TO

HEAVEN

& SLIDES BACK DOWN INTO MUD.

WE ARE SUCH A HEAVY BOOK THAT WE POUND TILES IF YOU

DROP US.

WE ARE NEVER DONE CRYING, LAUGHING, SPURTING, DYING:

ALL POLITICS ARE REDUCIBLE TO US.

WE ARE GOVERNED BY A WAVE CRUMBLING THE SHORES OF THE AMERICAS

& YOU DIGEST OUR BODY AS YOU READ,

ALL THE FEATHERS, SCALES, TEETH,

BREASTS, BLACK

MUDSLIDE GUNK.

LIKE THE GATORS UNDERNEATH NEW YORK

WE CLOG THE SEWERS OF LITERATURE.

WE MAKE FRIENDS WITH THE MOLE PEOPLE WHO TOSS RATS INTO OUR

BOOK-BODY.

RODENT CORPSES ROUND OUT THE FAT

UP OUR SLEEVES.

BREASTFED STARS MILKING DARKNESS

I ROSE WITH A MANGLED THROAT, I ROSE WITH THORNS PLANTED DEEP
INSIDE ME.

I COULD BARELY WHISPER "JUST DISSOLVE ME INTO AIRBORNE LIFE"—

A WIG OF ANA MARIA'S HAIR COVERED MY PUNCTURED BALDNESS.

LONG STRANDS TO TOSS BACK, RUN MY BILL THROUGH, BRAID, WHIP
ACROSS A BOY'S CHEST, COMB IN FRONT OF A MIRROR.

I DONNED THE WIG SO WIND HOWLED THROUGH MY PLUME DRESS & ANA
MARIA'S LOCKS AT THE SAME TIME.

FLYING, JUST THE TWO OF US, TWILIT BULBS GOD SQUEEZES OUT THE ASS
CHEEKS OF DAWN & NIGHT

WE WORE A BASEBALL CAP & THE HEAD OF A BABY GATOR BLOOMED ON IT.

"PREPARA TU ESQUELETO PARA EL AIRE"

ANA MARIA & I SLEEP WITH THE PHONE OFF THE HOOK. WE DREAM
TOGETHER AS TEENS. SHE DREAMS OF A STARTIP IN HER SIDE & RISES
WANTING TO GO SWIMMING. IN SACRED WIND THE BORDER TURNS INTO A
BIRD'S NIGHTMARE OR VEIN. A BIRD FORMS AN ENCLOSURE OF WOUNDS
BY INVITING 230 PAPER CUTS & NEVER BANDAGING THEM. IN V FORMATION A
BIRD UNRAVELS THE SKY, STAINS ITS BABY BLUE SURFACE, BOMBS THE
ARTIFICIAL DOME UNTIL NO COUNTRY IS SHRINKWRAPPED ANYMORE. ALL
MIGRANTS BLEED INTO CITIZENS BECAUSE OF A ROOST AMONG ANA MARIA'S
FAVORITE FRUIT: POMEGRANATES, OUR ORGANS EXPLODING. WHILE A
NECROPSY REGISTERS THE GATOR'S HEARTBEAT HOURS AFTER HE DIES,
NATIONAL GEOGRAPHIC NOTES THE TEARS OF CROCODILIANS AS THEY EAT.
ONLY MOTHER LORCA PENETRATES ME AS HARD AS THE GATOR & ANA MARIA.
HER GOLONDRINA SWERVES INTO MY CAGE OF FLESH HANGING OPEN LIKE A
JAW, FROTHING & BUBBLING IN THE GATOR'S IRISES.

LUCAS, THE FEELING YOU DESCRIBED AS "ALL I HAVE IS MYSELF" IS NEARLY REAL TO ME. I'M ANTICIPATING EXPERIENCING IT WHEN I MOVE NEXT YEAR, BECAUSE I PLAN ON MOVING AWAY FROM EVERY PERSON I KNOW. IT DOESN'T SURPRISE ME THAT YOU'VE ENCOUNTERED THIS FEELING BECAUSE YOU'VE MADE THIS MOVE (TO A FOREIGN LAND).

BLOOD BROTHERS (SHE WAS ALIVE)

I SPREAD BLOOD ROSES IN HER BED & SHE TOOK THE PETALS BACK TO MY

LOCKER

INSIDE MY TEXTBOOK THE ROSEPETALS DRIED OUT

CRIED OUT

MY BLOODTHIRST BURNED AS MUCH AS AN ALLIGATOR'S

THOUGH I WOULD NEVER KILL A BOY, I LONGED FOR THE TASTE OF BOYS'

NECKS

THOUGH BLOOD WAS MY CRAVING

IT SPILLED OUT AS FLECKED LILACS WHEN A BOY BROKE ANA MARIA'S HEART

& I SQUEEZED HER HAND

IF I GOT ANGSTY

I COULD ONLY COME UP WITH BODILESS METAPHORS IN A NOTEBOOK'S

MARGINS

THE METAPHOR OF "GOD" IS NOT WHAT I MEAN TO TARGET NOW

WITH MY BEAK

WITH MY BOOK

IT TOOK ANA MARIA TO MAKE ME UNDERSTAND

GOD'S NEED FOR BLOOD

WHEN SHE KISSED MY HAND IN THE HALLWAY IT WAS A MATTER OF

CIRCULATION

I WILL ALWAYS LOVE YOU,
ANA MARIA DE LIMA

THE BOOK IS RED

CHILDREN GAZE AT ANIMALS & SEE OUR SPECIAL FLOW OUT OF

CAGES.

THEY ASK QUESTIONS ABOUT SUBSTANCE.

THEIR SOFT MEAT LEAPS INTO THE AIR.

WARRIOR SPECIES,

ANA MARIA SAYS.

RINGWORMS THRIVING INSIDE THE BELLY OF THE BEAST,

THE GATOR SAYS.

LIKE THE GATOR, CHILDREN DECELERATE THEIR HEARTS TO 1 OR 2 BEATS

PER MINUTE.

THEY COULD DROWN THE BOOK UNDERWATER THANKS TO THEIR FOUR-

CHAMBERED ORGAN.

CHILDREN FLOCK ALL AROUND OUR BOOK BECAUSE

PREGNANCY SNAPS OUR SPINE

TENDER FLESH FILLS US OUT

WE ARE THE BOOK THAT WAS PASSED DOWN BONE-NAKED.

SPEAKING OF CHILDREN, TODAY A KID GUSHED CUPFULLS OF BLOOD INTO MY BARE HANDS.

THREEWAY ANAL COITUS

IF THE GATOR IS MY RIGHT WINGMAN & ANA MARIA IS MY LEFT

ALL THE PIECES OF

THE GATOR

ALL THE PIECES OF

ANA MARIA

ALL THE PIECES

SLIDE TOGETHER IN THE AIR ONCE I BREAK THE OLIVE TWIG IN MY BILL I GET

RID OF THE ANCHOR GAS BALLS CUM & SCREAM MY NAME A FLOOD OF

"LUCIUS, LUMINOUS, LIGHT" MY LOVES BECAUSE OF MUD BUBBLES IN MY

SOCKETS & THE BOOK'S SUCTION WE STAY ALOFT

CRUDE OIL SPURTS

EYEBALLS ROLL BACK

CONDENSATION TRAIL

HUMAN POET BEAT OUR EGG & SMACK OUR FACES WITH YOUR COCK

WE WHO LET YOU SPEAK AGAIN.

& THE DEAD DOVE WE ENCOUNTER ON THE SWAMP'S FRINGES HEWN

ONCE TO CLEAVE DIESEL PUFFS TWISTED NECK BENT BACK

OVER WAR FEATHERS TEEMING ANTS IN STYLISH DECAY, NOW WRENCHT

TO DIRECT ROADKILL BREEZE, THE DOVE'S IMPRINT ON LAND

A FRESH LETTER.

EAT THE DOVE'S HEART; OUR SHOCK DOCTRINE OF CYCLONE LOVE &

LEATHERY MEMBRANE AT THE GUNPOINT

OF A BOIL WE LANCE ON YOUR WRITHING TONGUE;

EAT THE DOVE'S HEART.

I WAS DEAD

UNTIL THE ROOM DIMMED.
I FLUTTERED OUT OF THE CIRCLE.
I DEFORMED THE CIRCLE BY EVACUATING ITS CENTER.
A GUST BLEW INTO MY BODY BAG & LIFTED THE RED FEATHERS I'D DROPPED.

THE BOLTED DOOR SWUNG WIDE OPEN

ON ANA MARIA, MY OLD FRIEND

THE GATOR, MY NEW FRIEND.

I PUSHED THE PERIMETER OF THE CIRCLE OUTWARD WHEN I FLEW TOWARD IT.
I STRETCHED ITS ELASTIC CIRCUMFERENCE THE WAY A HAND
TAUTENS A BEDSHEET,
THE WAY A PLANE DRAGS OUT A CLOUD.

I LANDED ON ANA MARIA'S MAIMED FINGER.
I HEARD HER LAUGH BECAUSE THE POET HAD SURVIVED.
NO CANDLES BLEW OUT.
NO ONE INTERRUPTED THE CEREMONY.

THE BOOK,
SO THRILLED TO BE IN THE SAME CIRCLE AS OUR
CONGREGATING BODIES,

LEAPT OFF THE SHELF.

LUCAS, DO YOU EVER FEEL LIKE YOU HAVE ME? I MEAN WHEN YOU GET TO FEELING ALONE, DO YOU EVER CONSIDER ME? I KNOW WE'RE FAR AWAY FROM EACH OTHER DAILY. AND I'VE FELT YOU HOLD BACK WITH ME BEFORE... YOU DON'T FEEL THE NEED TO TELL ME EVERYTHING, RIGHT?

CAVATINA OF CRYSTALS

MIRED IN MUD & TURBID WATERS, UNCLASPED TALONS ON

THE OZONE ENCRUSTED IN CARTILAGE, STRANDED FISH HUNG

FROM MY BILL, A PELICAN'S SOLO RIPPLED OUT TO THE FREEWAY OR

A MESSAGE IN A BOTTLE INSTEAD OF

A SHELL

BARE

IS THE BOOK'S THROAT

THE READER WILL BITE LIKE A PENIS

WILL DIP INTO MAMMAL MELT

ANA MARIA'S EARSPLITTING THOUSAND-YARD

SUN-STARE

ECHOLOCATES A THIRSTY TIDE OF BATS

THE BOOK REGENERATES SCRAPS OF PLAIN SKIN

THE BOOK BLOWS ME INTO A COFFIN & I HEAR MUFFLED SLAVES RIP LEAVES

OVERHEAD THEY CLING TO THE SWAMP'S CANOPY BECAUSE THEY NEVER

THUDDED LIKE MY WORM-BALLOONED BODY FLAPPING CRUSHING ENSNARED

TALONS SCREECHING AT MOSS THUNDERHEADS BILLOW IN THE FIRMAMENT

FROM A MANGROVE DOME UNDERWATER MY FRIENDS CAN'T SEE

PRESSURIZED FLUORESCENT PREENING NO LONGER A WHEEZE ONE SOARS

WITH THE BOOK DRIPPING LIKE A WINDOW BATTERING MY BIRDFACE IN

MOCKERY OF

EARRINGS OF TEARS TWINKLING UP THERE

OUR BOOK IS ESCAPED AS A BIRD OUT OF THE SNARE OF FLOWERS: THE SNARE IS BROKEN, AND WE ARE ESCAPED.

THE BURNING

THE GATOR SITS BY THE RED HEART OF A TORCH ALMOST ASPHYXIATED; OUT OF THE BOOK HE GLOWS AS WE'RE ALL RAKED ABLAZE; FLAMES LICK & SPIT AT MY HEIGHT & DROWN OUT WARNING SQUAWKS; I BLAST A GUST ON SCALES BUT TURTLES CAN'T INHALE IN SHELLS; A VULTURE WITH THE EYESIGHT OF A KNIFE I STAB A CARCASS IN THE GATOR HOLE; THE WORD BECAME FLESH ASHEN & BLOODY IN THE PITS; CORPSE STRETCHING SMOULDERING MARSHLAND & PINELAND CRACKLING BIG SPLATTERS OF YOLK

OH MY GOD

OR ANA MARIA

SWIRL US AROUND ELEMENTAL CENSORS

THE WAY A SCAVENGER CIRCLES

BLACK BARS SEARED ONTO LAND

DEATH OF THE BOOK

BIRD, FASTEST LIVING THING IN AIR, CLOSEST TO JESUS, FOLD INTO THE

BOOK WHENEVER LIGHTNING

STRIKES;

SHIT GETS STICKY;

DRONE, TWIRL UP HIGH, WIELD BLADES, SURVEIL THE WIGS & LUNGS OF

THE BOOK;

THE BIRD LIGHTS A CIGARETTE & INFLATES A MUTE THROAT BUBBLE;

HANDICAPPED BOOK, COLLAPSE ON MY BACK

SO A DUMB LOON SINS WITH YOU;

EACH SHIT STAIN I TRANSLATE INTO CLUCKS PERCHED ON DWARF

CYPRESSES UNTIL

THE SNAP OF THEIR LEXICON;

CRY, TREK FROM FACE TO FACE IN THE WET LAND, PLUCK KERATIN

TO SKELETON THE BOOK

IN POSTMORTAL GARB;

RIBBONS OF FLESH, COMMUNE WITH STARS AS I FALL & BLOTCH IN

OUR YELLOWING, FUCK WITH

OUR BONES

ANA MARIA PUSHED HARD SHELLS INTO MY SKIN

& FLIPPED ON AN EVOLUTIONARY FEEDBACK LOOP

SO I WOULD BURST INTO ANTHEM

AT MIDNIGHT

THOUGH I BATHED INSIDE GATOR HOLES, GURGLING NOTES

WEREN'T ENOUGH

FOR OUR HOT PINK FLAG TO TATTER ALL THE TIME

A THRUSH MUMMY ON A LOTUS FLOWER, I'M SWARMING

WITH BABY GATORS

WHERE THE BOOK HAD BEEN BORN

SO YOU'LL IMAGINE

TALONS GLUED TO A FOSSIL IN ANA MARIA'S PALMS

THE GATOR WEEPS LUMPS OF COAL OVER HER SHOULDER

"O, BOOK"

O, BOOK

SCREAM FOR THE NATION

NOT ONLY AM I BLIND TO THE TRIANGLE YOU WEDGED OPEN

NOBODY HEARS THE ECHO

YOU FLESHED OUT OF MY CICATRIX

OK. Who would like to begin?

I can start. I thought the strength of this was that it's a very gutsy and unusual project, and the request is relatively modest considering that he's planning two months of writing time. It's conceivable that he needs to go to this place in order to flesh out this project. So that's good for me.

The writing, however, I can take issue with. It seems melodramatic. And it seems to me that the violence of the subject matter—he's already noted how corporate media has made a spectacle out of it—it seems to me that he's not doing justice to his friend. I think that the subject matter could be better served with a cooler treatment. I'm more interested in learning about this person than the details with the alligator and so on. And forgive me—it almost seems cartoonish. Maybe intentionally at times, but sometimes unintentionally so. So that's it for me. I like the project, I don't care much for the poems.

I agree with all you said about the work. The positive thing I found in it—the descriptive details were very, very strong. To the point that I don't know anything about the person involved. I get much more of the theme, and as you said, the images of tragedy are very strong, and somewhere along the line we need to know this person.

Yes.

I don't feel like I know Ana Maria at all.

The writer has a relationship—an imaginary and imaginative relationship with the alligator that's way more energetic than the relationship with the friend who was killed, and I think it borders on the bizarre. In fact, it doesn't just border, it is bizarre. It's bizarre.

In a bad way?

I believe in a bad way, yes. I think it's quite inappropriate. And I don't think it successfully does what he's trying to do. I don't think he knows what he's trying to do. He thinks he's trying to recover the dignity of his lost friend, but I think he's fallen into a reverie about being an alligator. If that were deliberate, and you took the dead friend out of the scene and sort of put it off to the side and said, you know, I'm going to write—

A mind-meld with an alligator?

Yeah, that could be an interesting project, but I don't think that for his stated project it's effective.

I think he's appropriating her the same way that he's complaining about others doing, I felt.

It's also very strange to have an entire manuscript on this one moment.

Exactly.

I agree.

And I think the fact that the one friend doesn't exist outside of this moment, for me at least, I would have a hard time reading an entire—

I agree with you. I noted two or three times that very issue. And when I looked at the impact in Minnesota—"I envision holding the workshops in a range of settings… natural history museum, libraries, and zoos"—I don't see how the manuscript is going to match that in any shape or form.

I mean, if you could pull it off that would be great.

But it would have to be different material than this. You know you're not going to read "My egghead, I cry yolky tears in the boat while my father frowns at me" in a natural history museum and have that be an effective thing.

I think that there were moments in the poems—let me see what I said—I said, "There were nicely surprising moments and the poems were mostly competent, but in quite a few places they were very prosy and flat." I'm looking at the first one on page 135—"The Killspot Eggs Me On." I think the reason I don't engage in terms of craft is because there are very long lines that seem to end arbitrarily—a second line ends on a "the"—and then a third line is one word that just sits there all alone. And that happens again and again. For a word to sit all alone on a line like that it has to have so much power. So much purpose. But I'm not seeing that always in these poems. I think maybe that's what's turning these poems into less than what he intends them to be for his friend.

So in terms of content but also in terms of execution.

In execution of the poems, I think he's undercutting what he hopes to do for her.

I think I had a more positive reaction to the poems, but I do think that what you point out about the line breaks is a sort of consistent struggle I had.

I do like it. I like the concept. I think it's cool to take a private grief and play it out in a way that has ecological consequences or ramifications.

And more mythic, I think. In some ways what I'm seeing is a lot more mythic than ecological as such.

What he's wanting to say is that the threat to gators is causing these attacks. That's where he intends to go with this manuscript.

Well, and I think possibly, the fact that there isn't as much science or ecology in there is a lack of knowledge on his part, and that's part of why he's going—he's going to research those things.

And that makes sense. But I wonder if it's too premature to say that he'll have a completed book by 2012.

It's not just the science that's lacking, the grief is lacking. And I think he's being mastered a bit by his own subject. Maybe a little bit by ambition, although maybe that's a dangerous supposition to make, but yeah, let's hear about this woman, the relationship, and the grief, and then you can tell me about alligators.

Does this applicant meet all three criteria—artistic quality, merit and feasibility of plan, impact or benefit to the state, and/or creative community?

Please raise your hand if you agree.

I'll say yes.

One yes?

I'll say yes too.

Two yesses.

Please raise your hand if you do not agree.

Four no's. Please draw a line through this one.

ANA MARIA, HOW WILL I REBIRTH THE BOOK ON MY OWN & BECOME YOUR

AVE MARIA

LUCAS, I WISH WE COULD SPEAK! I WANT TO TELL YOU THESE THINGS, BADLY. BUT I WORRY THAT I'M JUST WRITING A BOOK ABOUT MYSELF, WHICH YOU MAY PREFER TO PUT BACK ON THE SHELF.

I STAGE A SUPERFLIGHT

& MULTIPLY.

ALL MY OILY FEATHERS TURN GOLD.

UPON CLIFFS WHERE I WAS BANISHED FROM THE BOOK, I LAUNCH OUT

OF BROKEN EGGS.

MY NUMBERS RISE UNCHECKED.

IN A CLOUD ALL REPLICAS OF ME

DASH TO & FRO, WHIRLING WITH THE RUSH OF A WAND IN THE WIND.

THERE IS A CLATTER OF GILDED PIGEON WINGS

VS.

A VULTURE FLIPPED ON ITS BACK.

ALL THE LUCASES CASCADE AGAINST THE MOON, OUR NAKED BIRDWATCHER,

WHILE STARS ALIGN THEMSELVES AS

THE FACE OF THE GATOR.

MY DEAR EVERYTHING, I PAGE THE GATOR

IN A SENTENCE OF TURDS.

MY DEAR AIRPUFF, THE GATOR WRITES BACK AS

A TIRED CONSTELLATION.

I CLOAK THE SKY BECAUSE THE GATOR WRITES BACK

I EXHAUST CLOUDS THAT WISPEN LIKE THE GATOR

WHO SUSURRATES WITH THE BOOK

i have to disappear now

your eggs were never defective

they were loaded with the blood

of a gay earth mother

a bird flattened into a page

& rounded out as a bullet

your blood is ours even if we stop

throbbing

don't you remember what ana maria wrote

on that cold night

we were all alive

YOU ARE EMBEDDED IN ME THE WAY A SEED IS IN A MELON.

RECOMPOSITION

ANTS, BEETLES & CENTIPEDES DISAPPEAR INTO WOOD, LEAVING

MOUNDS AS BURIAL SITES

I WANT TO DIG UP. I AM THE LONELIEST, GAUNTEST STORK

PERCHED ON ROOTS

DISLODGED BY MY OWN HURRICANE. OUT OF THE LAST DRIP OF BLOOD

THAT MULTI-

TASKED VIA WINGS

PETALS COAGULATE

IN

A CORSAGE.

MANGROVE SEEDS CROSS WITH FUNGAL WORDS

BLOATING WITH GAS ROUND THE SUPPLEJACK'S TORTUOUS

WRIST

THE GATOR MAN

QUICKSAND BURPS OUT A MAN INFECTED WITH SCALES.

IT'S NOT JUST

A GATORHEAD CONSTRICTING HIS SCREAM.

TO UNWRAP INVASIVE SNAKES PIERCING HIM IS

TO DOT THE LAND'S VERDANCY. SAWGRASS

MARKS ON HIS ANKLES EMULATE

LUCASES ADMINISTERED IN CHOPPED WOOD. BUT THE

MAN WILTS WITHOUT SLOW DRUGS OR THE BOOK'S SELF-ANNIHILATING

CREED.

SO BLURRED IS HIS DYING MY WINGS FILL IN

SHROUDS OF MIST. AMID HIS JAWS PETALLING FOAM

THE GLASS OF FANGS

HITS ME

UNDER A BROMELIAD'S CRIMSON SPIKES

HE OPENS HIS EYES TO FORBIDDEN FRUIT

A GHOST ORCHID WITH DEEPLY CLEFT FLOWERS SWAYS NEAR US

A BENDED CYPRESS SLIDES BACK INTO MUD CLUMPS ON ITS KNEES

THE GATOR MAN WON'T EJECT ME HELLWARD DESPITE MY BIRD FLU

I THINK I'M THE WRITER WHO DIES BEFORE FINISHING A BOOK & DEPRIVES

HER PAGES OF

A SPINAL CORD

WATCH THE GATOR MAN CRADLE ME & LIPSYNCH SPOTLIT

if the book is your baby mine is the sculpture of raw meat i made before dying of aids

THIS IS A TIME WHEN I AM MOST VUNERABLE TO ANYTHING. I CAN EASILY MAKE PARALLELS TO THE TEXT WITH MY OWN PERSONAL EXPERIENCE.

FLAMING CREATURES

WE TWIRL IN THE CENTER OF THE SWAMP, A ROSE IN THE GATOR MAN'S

JAWS, STEM ROUGED WITH LIPSTICK.

A TECHNICOLOR PINK IN HIS EYES, HE SPINS FASTER THAN MY WHIRLWIND.

OTHER QUEENS AROUND US, DECKED OUT IN PLUMAGE BORROWED

FROM PONDS,

HARK BACK IN SWAN DRAG TO MY BEST FRIEND.

ONCE EVERYONE FAINTS EXCEPT THE GATOR MAN & I

& AN OPOSSUM'S TAIL LETS GO OF A LIMB

I LIFT MY MENDED WING &

BRIM LIKE SPARKLING WATER.

I WALTZ WITH THE GATOR MAN WHILE GRAY CLOUDS GATHER.

THE SKY CRACKLES UNDER THE CLOUDS,

ERUPTING WHITE LIGHT

THAT TEACHES US TO FLASH LIKE ANA MARIA'S CLEAVAGE.

I DON'T WANT TO GET MARRIED, I SING ALOUD.

I WANT TO CONSTELLATE IN BLACK BLOOD WITH MY CO-STARS.

TO BLOT OUT THE ORANGE SUN

WE'LL BURN IN THE NOVA OF A DETONATING BREAST.

WE ARE JUST NOW BECOMING FUCKING LOVERS.

SECRETE

I FIRST CAME OUT TO ANA MARIA SHE WARNED ME ABOUT DADDIES WITH
AIDS BLEEPED-OUT PRICK & ROT SPLATTERING RED INK PAPERCUT WE
EXTEND IN A BUBBLING CREEK CONDOM I PECK AS THE STREWN LITTER OF

THE GATOR   THE GATOR MAN

ME   & ANA MARIA

REPEAT

AS ANA MARIA OPENS MY CAGE SHE OPENS MY FACE; MY BILL PROTRUDES INTO THE GAP OF HER BREASTS WHILE THEY RADIATE UPON A FOUR-CORNERED PAGE; HER AREOLAS SPRAY A PROTEINED GLAZE VIA

THIS COCKED PLUME PEN

BASICALLY, I SEE HIM AS VERY MUCH STUCK IN THE PUPAL STAGE.

"ANA MARIA"

VACANT MOUTH AJAR, SILENT SHOUT IN MY EAR.

LIKE A TORN SHEET ON A LINE, THE GATOR MAN LIVES ON A PRAYER.

IF I SPLAYED MYSELF ON HIS STATUESQUE PLATES & GAVE HIM MY ORGANIC

MATTER TO MOLD,

HE'D STILL LONG FOR SPEECH.

THEN HE WOULD CRY MY SHIT RIGHT OFF OF HIM.

WHILE HE LEAVES HIS SERRATED SNOUT OPEN, I BUILD A NEST OF TWIGS &

FOIL ON HIS HEAD.

SOMETHING WE CAN'T SEE, WHOSE FACE WE DON'T KNOW, STRAINS TO BE

BORN IN BETWEEN MILKWEED &

THE GATOR MAN'S DISEASE.

WHAT IF I READ THE GATOR MAN'S LIPS WITH A KISS.

WHAT IF WE TRIED SOUL-MAKING BY UTTERING ONE NAME FOR HIS DEATH

& MY LIFE

TWO WORDS

& OUR SEED INSIDE THEM.

LAST NIGHT I ATE SHROOMS.

I CAME UP WITH A NAME:

MARKUS AKUREYRI

THE LAST PART OF THE NAME MAY NOT BE PART OF THE NAME—IT'S A LOCATION.

MUSEUM IN THE MANGROVE DOME

RIVERS OF LAVA

CLAY FIGURINES TIED TO ROOTS

AN EFFIGY OF THE GATOR MAN DRESSED AS A HIPPIE IN A TOMB

A CRUCIFIX COSTUMED WITH ANTS

SAINTS WITH ANIMAL HEADS

A RIMBAUD MASK I TRY ON

MY BEAK TEARS A HOLE THROUGH IT

THE WORD "MOTHER" PAINTED WITH A COMMA NEXT TO IT

TEENAGE BOYS SMOOCHING A WORLD MAP

FOUR RED HANDPRINTS ON A NEWSPAPER COLORED OVER

WOVEN THROUGH A BOOK, STRANDS OF HUMAN HAIR

THOUSANDS OF FIREFLIES PULSATING

SINCE THE DAY EACH ARTIST DIED

GRACE THEIR ART LIKE EYESHINE

SINCE THE TRANSFORMATION OF THE GATOR MAN ON THE NIGHT

HIS CELLS BLASTED OFF

CHEEKS WRACKED BY SCALES

TO GAZE AT NEW YORK CITY FROM A CLIFF

WAS TO DROP INTO THAT GREEN MAW

THE SHIMMER OF ANA MARIA

HAVING PINNED TO BARK THE NOTE

"PAINTING: MAN WITH BIRD IN CHEST IN PLACE OF HEART"

FIRE IN MY BELLY

IN THE WET LAND OF ACIDIC, PEATY SOIL, THE PLOP OF MY DROPPINGS

BINDS

ME & THE WETNESS.

A DRY COLD HOLE EXPANDS INSIDE THE GATOR MAN, BLACKENING HIS

TONGUE

SO IT STICKS OUT.

I FILL HIS THROAT FROM UP HIGH WITH

SEEDY SPECKLED DISCHARGE, MY BELLY HOT FROM ITS ACCUMULATION OF

ART.

AS BODIES MATERIALIZE, EFFLORESCING OUT OF GOBS, THEY ACT UP

INSIDE THE GATOR MAN.

THEY DECORATE HIS ENTRAILS WITH RIPPLES OF BLOOD ROSES.

UNDER SCALES

BLOSSOM

THE GATOR PEOPLE;

PETALS ON OUR VIRAL TREE OF LIFE.

"I WON'T LIVE UNTIL YOU LAY AN EGG IN EVERLASTING TESTIMONY TO OUR CURRENT OF BLOOD."

IMAGINE THE GATOR MAN TALKING

IN HIS FEVERDREAM, DRAPED AT TIMES IN A SOPPING RAG, AT TIMES IN A

SOGGY ROSE.

MY BALD EAGLE'S SCREECH

IS A VERSION OF HIS SPIT, WARPED BY THE DIMENSIONS OF THIS FILTHY

SKY.

BUT I HAVE ANA MARIA TO BLOW HAIR UNDER

MY WINGBEAT I KEEP

A PREGNANT RACCOON IN MIND TO

GRAZE A POOL OF BLOOD

IN A LANDFILL EVEN IF SOMEONE FLIPS THE BIRD THIS BITCH GOES

ON BEDEWING HER STOMACH A CUNTY SWAN

MY NEST IN GARBAGE PINKSTAINED MAMMATUS CLOUDS

PUMELLING OVALS INTO RECTANGLES AS IF A ROUNDNESS COULD

WHITEN NIGHT &

BAPTIZE US IN HER NAME

OPEN UP YOUR MOUTH
EAT ME LOVE
OPEN UP
ME OPEN
ME EAT
OPEN YOUR MOUTH
ME LOVE YOUR MOUTH
MOUTH LOVE
ME EAT YOUR MOUTH
YOUR OPEN MOUTH
OPEN LOVE
EAT ME UP
OPEN ME
MOUTH UP

GAY EARTH MOTHER

DREAM OF A GATOR BOY & MORPH INTO A ROBIN MY ORANGE BELLY
GARLANDED WITH LES FLEURS DU MAL A COKE CAN SHOVED INSIDE MY
BILL CLICK WING FEATHERS & BLAST A RIFLE BIRD'S KILLER FLARE UPON
THE STITCHED LIPS OF THE GATOR BOY STAB ME YES—MY NIPPLES SO
LACERATED THEY PUFF WITH HIS FETID GASP JUST AS ANA MARIA'S
CHEST WOULD HAVE GLITTERSTREAMING INTO HIS SUCKLE TEETH-RIDDEN AS

THE FLOOD GATOR PEOPLE DROWN IN THE FLOCK THEY DIE FOR

LAY THE GATOR BOY'S SCALES OUT FOR AIR OVER MY DEAD BODY
REGANITES SNIP IN A SMOG-VAULT WRIGGLE WORMS DOWN TO HIS LUNGS &
MAKE

"SILENCE" = BREATH

WHEN RICK MORANIS WAS GETTING A MASK MADE OF HIM FOR SOMETHING IN HONEY I SHRUNK THE KIDS, HE GOT CLAUSTROPHOBIC AND TORE THE MASK OFF 3 TIMES BEFORE GETTING FINISHED. HE COULDN'T CALM DOWN UNTIL HE HAD A JOINT. A GUEST 3-D DESIGN TEACHER TOLD ME THIS BECAUSE HE WAS THE ONE PUTTING THE MASK ON HIM.

BUG-CHASER

CAGED LIKE A PARROT, THE GATOR MAN BOBS AT MY CROCODILE TEARS,

BLOODY EMERALDS UNDER MY LIDS;

ACROSS MY CHEST, ONE BULLET-SHAPED DESIGN

OF RESPLENDENT HUES;

AGAINST A FAÇADE OF VELVET ASH CURTAINS, I LIE IN BED;

FROM THE GATOR MAN'S JAWS & THE GATE OF HIS CAGE, REAMS OF PAPER

ROLL

UNSPOOLING BEYOND MY STATURE OF LACE, VEILS & BEADS;

FOR MONTHS I FEAR I AM POZ,

THE BOOK'S UNWINKING EYES ON THIS STAGE RIFE

WITH TERMITES, OR;

I PLAY DEAD IN RIFLE RANGE WITH THE GATOR MAN,

BITCHES OF IMPOSSIBILITY, WE ARE.

SAY A PRAYER,
A.M.

SOUL-STUDDED LASH

PLEASE FACE A TAUT SILHOUETTE ABOVE THE WHIP OF THE BOOK'S

UMBILICAL CORD ON YOUR EAR.

WITH THE STOOPED KNEES OF CYPRESSES

GO DOWN ON & CREAM INTO THE NIGHTS I, PLUMELESS, DO NOT RIM THE

BOOK.

STARS ARE CAVITIES WHOSE FLOW SMOTHERS OUR CHEEKS NOW;

DIRTY LIGHT ONLY LICKS US IF THE BOOK CRYSTALLIZES

AS A CHICKEN HEART ATHROB AT YOUR FINGERTIPS, VEINS REINCARNATED

FROM THE GATOR MAN'S TONGUE

INSERTING THE SUN WHERE IT BECOMES

LARVAL RAIN IN YOUR ANAL SKY, A JOLT OF RAINBOW OUT OF YOUR TRACT;

ALL GATEWAY MEN

GET FISTED ON A SLING.

THE ANNUNCIATION

WINGS OF SEVERED HANDS PLUCK THE GATOR MAN SO LIKE A STEM IN

THE EPICENTER

WE CLUTCH EACH OTHER WITH LITTLE JERKS HEADS RATTLING FROM THE

SKYSCRAPE

OUR BRAINS LAND IN THE SEASON OF HIS PEOPLE'S DROOPING

OUR LADIES OF FLOWERS WHO CRAWLED UNDER BEDS TO FERTILIZE A GOTH

BOUQUET

A WHITEWASHED DRAG QUEEN'S ANGELIC CROAKING

WHERE THE GATOR MAN'S INNER EAR THRUMS I SUCK ON PLATED SKIN LIKE A

PAINTED NAIL

ORGANS SASHAY OUTSIDE OUR BLINDING ORB EGGS IN OUR MOUTHS

AIMED AT A NIGHTMARISH QUAKE OF BODIES CRESTING

WE TAP SHELLS WE DROOL THE SPARKLE OF PISS

WE KISS & MY LYMPH NODES BUD IN WAIT FOR THORNS TO LIVE IN US

LUCAS,

IS THERE ANY WAY YOU COULD GIVE ME A FEW PEARLS OF ADVICE ON MY ARTIST STATEMENT? I JUST WROTE IT NOW AND I'M GOING TO BED WITHOUT FEELING VERY GOOD ABOUT IT. I KNOW IT'S NOT DONE, BUT PLEASE, IF YOU HAVE A MINUTE, MAKE COMMENTS.

IN MY WORK, I JUXTAPOSE THE EXPERIENCE OF HUMAN DECAY—SYMBOLIZED BY A GIANT TOOTH—WITH VAST, UNTAMED LANDSCAPES. I USE THE TOOTH AS A MONUMENT TO SELF-DESTRUCTION. BY FLANKING THE MONUMENT WITH NATURE, I REFER TO THE PRIMORDIAL HISTORY OF HUMAN DEVOTION TO THIS EXPERIENCE. HUMAN SACRIFICES, FOOT BINDING, AND POTLATCH CEREMONIES ARE ALL EXAMPLES.

BENDITA TÚ ERES I PRAY WITH MOSQUITOS A PRAYER FOR THE FACELESS WHERE ANA MARIA
BLED

THE GATOR MAN IS BROUGHT TO HIS KNEES IN LIGHT OF THE DIRT ON HIS FACE.

ONCE IT CRUMBLES WITH THE EARTH HIS FACE SPURTS A RAINBOW.

BECAUSE A GATOR'S MUSCLES CONTRACT FOR DAYS AFTER DEATH SO DO THE

GATOR MAN'S.   HE STROKES HIS RIDGED PENIS & SHOOTS CUM AT THE SUN FROM

A CREEK-BANK WHERE ANA MARIA WAS SHED

CONCEPTUALLY, I AM INFLUENCED BY THE WRITTEN WORKS OF GEORGES BATAILLE—ESPECIALLY HIS NOVEL "STORY OF THE EYE" AND THE SHORT STORY "MY MOTHER." THESE PIECES CENTER AROUND CHARACTERS WHO NEED SELF-ANNIHILATION.

ALLIGATOR COALITION TO UNLEASH POWER

WATERWARD MY FRAME TOO PAPERY FOR MY INFLATED BREAST I'M LINED

WITH THORNY TEETH AS THE GATOR MAN SNAPS ME OFF & TIPS INTO THE

DILATING EYES OF THE SPRINGHEAD PANSIES BESIEGING THE SCUM HE & I

BARE OUR ROSEATE FLESH TO

THE BLOOD OF THE GATOR &

I AM FOND OF WORKING WITH STONES BECAUSE THEY ARE OFTEN VERY HEAVY AND BODY-LIKE. THE TEETH I DRAW TAKE ON STONE CHARACTERISTICS—

ANA MARIA ANA

MARIA ANA

MARIA

THE BOOK IS A CRACK (A CLOACAL KISS)

A STONE HURLED AT THE BLUE SCREEN OF THE CREEK LETS THE GATOR MAN & I THRASH AS WET FRIENDS

THE RED FEATHER ON MY ANUS IS A GASHED WOMB FLASHING THE SIGN *IT'S LIKE THE 80'S: ANY FRIENDS*

NOT DYING ARE ALREADY DEAD

PUS-FILLED LUNGS SHARDS OF CHRIST ALL OVER OUR KISS GLASS STAINING OUR THROATS ETCH ORIFICES

FOR ANA MARIA

SHE WHO BLISTERS THROUGH ANY SHELL

WRESTED FROM THE MIRROR OF ACID RAINWATER ANA MARIA UNKNOTS THE GATOR MAN'S TONGUE &

ENTERS OUR VEINS

OH LUCAS, DON'T HESITATE TO POUR YOURSELF OUT RIGHT NOW.

FRESH SCABS UP HIGH, THE GATOR MAN ULULATES

UNMUSCLED MARYS, WE

NEEDED A BIRD BRAIN TO HOOK ONTO FROM THE AQUEOUS MASS OF A LONG CRIMSON TRAIL IN MUCK

ROPED WEIGHT TOSSED DOWN TO PULP THE BOOK PRIED APART THE COFFINS OF QUEENS

SCALY PLUMED CHILDREN LIMPED OUT NOT TOO SICK FOR BREAST STROKES ACROSS THE SWAMP

LIMP-WRISTED UNDER THE PAGE WE PERFUMED A GATOR'S ENTRAILS TAKING OVOID FORM

IN CADAVERIC BREEZE WE MARYS SUTURED TO A BELLY PUNCTURED BY THE VIRUS

SPLASHING THE YOLKBLOOD OF THE GATOR'S FACE YOU ATE

WE ALL ATE IT

EVEN ANA MARIA LOST HER HANDS TASTING THE GATOR

SHE SLICED US WITH HIS LINE OF SIGHT

HOLEY CURTAIN DROP

I TOO AM A QUEEN WEARING HER CORONET OF PEARLS

MY CROWN DOES NOT FALL ASHORE & SHATTER AMID OUR CORPSES HEWN OF PETALS

MY PEARLS SUSTAIN THEIR FLUORESCENCE FOR YOU ANA MARIA

I RAISE MY BEAK FOR YOUR GATOR & MY GATOR MAN EVEN AFTER DIPPING THE TIP IN A BLOODBATH

I CAN LIFT MY BEAK LIKE A MAST IN THE MIDST OF THE STARS BULLETS & BITCHES WE SUMMON TO TRASH &

CONDENSE INTO ONE SEVERED GREEN TAIL WRAPPED

TIGHT AROUND OUR BONES TILL

THE BOOK LETS DOWN HAIR

THE SWAMP WASHED & DRAINED BY BOILING BLOOD WITH MEAT SCRAPS

A DEEP DARK PITCH CONVULSING LIGHT AROUND YOUR NAME ABSORBS THE SKY OF SHRIEKS

WE DRAG OUT

PS–I DON'T REMEMBER EXACTLY WHAT I GOT TO TELL YOU ABOUT MY EXPERIENCE (PROBABLY JUST THAT BAD END OF IT), BUT IT REALLY WAS AMAZING. TRULY. THE SENSATION WAS BEYOND BELIEF. EVERYONE TOUCHED ME—I FELT LIKE AN ISLAND COVERED IN VOLCANOES.

SARAH FOX AND BHANU KAPIL NURTURED THIS BOOK INTO BEING. MY DEEPEST GRATITUDE TO THEM,

A.T. GRANT, MARIA DAMON, FENG SUN CHEN, JOHANNES GÖRANSSON, JOYELLE MCSWEENEY, PAUL CUNNINGHAM, ANDREW SHUTA, JOSIE RAWSON, JULIE SCHUMACHER, RYAN MURPHY, JESSE LEANEAGH, DANIEL LUEDTKE, ALEX SMITH, PATRICK MARTIN, MY MFA CLASSMATES,

AND MY FAMILY.

THANK YOU NICK, CLAUDIA, AND MARIANNE FOR YOUR FRIENDSHIP IN THE FOREST WHERE WE, TOO, SANG.

SELECTIONS FROM WET LAND HAVE PREVIOUSLY APPEARED IN GOBBET, CULTURESTRIKE, AND THE CHAPBOOK GHOSTLINES (RADIOACTIVE MOAT PRESS).